HAIR-RAISING TALES

retold by
Corinne Denan
illustrated by
Meredith Lightbown

Troll Associates

Hair-Raising Tales: Masque of the Red Death, Poe; *Bluebeard*, Perrault.

Copyright © 1980 by Troll Associates, Mahwah, N.J.

Library of Congress# 79-66334
ISBN 0-89375-334-3/0-89375-333-5 (pb)

CONTENTS

Masque of the Red Death

The Red Death was moving about the land. No one was safe. No killer had ever been so feared or so horrible.

The Red Death struck quickly, without warning. The victims felt sharp pains and dizziness at first. But then came the true horror for which the thing was named. The victims would begin to bleed. It was terrible. It was as if the skin suddenly opened, and blood leaked from every pore. No one could bear to watch as people fell to the floor, shrieking in agony. Within half an hour, they would be dead. Their faces were scarlet with blood, for this was the mark of the Red Death.

No one knew what caused it. No one knew how to cure it. And no one knew where it would strike next. The people lived in constant terror and torment.

But there was one who seemed not to fear the Red Death at all. His name was Prince Prospero. Wealthy and lighthearted, he continued his life of pleasure even as people dropped to their deaths around him. The Prince seemed hardly to notice.

The Red Death continued to stalk the land. At last, even the Prince could see that half his servants had died, as well as many of his friends.

Instead of showing fear or sorrow, the Prince reacted in his usual way. "I shall have a great party," he said. "A six-month party that will make us forget this dreadful annoyance."

And so, Prince Prospero invited hundreds of the knights and ladies of the court. "We shall get away from this depressing city," he told them. "We shall leave for my castle in the country."

The knights and ladies were only too happy to follow the Prince to his estate in a secluded part of the land. Perhaps here they could forget the Red Death.

Prince Prospero's castle was splendid. But it was lonely and eerie, too. A strong high wall with iron gates surrounded the entire estate. And once all the guests had entered, the Prince had the gates locked and welded shut. "To keep out the Red Death," he said with a laugh. "Let the rest of the world look out for itself." And his friends agreed.

Inside the castle, the Prince had stocked provisions for a long stay. There were all kinds of food and drink. There were servants to care for the guests' every need. There were musicians for concerts, and ballet dancers for other evening entertainment. There were books to read and clowns to make people laugh. It seemed the perfect way to wait until the horror on the outside had ended. Here, within the castle walls, everyone was safe and happy and secure.

The party went on for nearly six months. From time to time, the Prince received word that the Red Death raged over the land even more furiously than before. But nothing touched the merrymakers inside the castle. They laughed and danced and feasted throughout their days.

But even merrymaking can become boring after a time. So the Prince had a new idea. "A masked ball," he told his guests. "We shall have a great masked ball, and all will attend."

The Prince's guests were delighted with the idea. There was much excitement as the knights and ladies decided upon the proper costumes to wear to such a splendid affair. Soon all was ready, and the masked ball began.

For this grand occasion, the Prince had decided to use seven ballrooms in the old wing of the castle. The rooms were in a row, one after the other, their tall narrow windows looking out, not on the countryside, but on a closed hallway. All the rooms were lighted with fiery torches placed

in holders on the wall. The effect was strange and startling.

Each room was painted a different color, with long velvet drapes and tapestries to match. The first room was blue, the second purple, the third green, the fourth orange, the fifth white, and the sixth violet. Strangest of all, the panes in the tall, narrow windows were made of stained glass that matched the colors of the walls.

"What a quaint idea," said one of the ladies. "The Prince has very unusual taste."

But it was the seventh room that the guests found most unusual. For here, the walls were shrouded in black. Long, thick tapestries of black velvet reached down to the dark carpet. In this room, the windows did not match the black of the walls. Instead, they were a deep blood-red.

This seventh room was strange in one other way, too. Against one wall stood a giant clock made of dark ebony. Its heavy gold pendulum swung back and forth with a dull sound. But when it struck the hour, the sound that came forth was so eerie and odd that the dancers grew pale and stopped in the middle of their steps. The musicians held their violin bows poised in the air and looked nervously at one another. They vowed that the next chiming of the clock would not make them feel such dread. Yet each time the hour drew near, they became strangely uneasy again.

But, even with the strange, dark ballroom and the strange-sounding clock, the masked ball was a scene of great gaiety. The dancers in their costumes seemed to float beneath the flickering candles. Laughter and talk filled the first six rooms. But none of the guests would return to the seventh room after they had seen it.

Prince Prospero seemed to be enjoying himself more than anyone else. But that was his way. "Are you having a pleasant time?" he would ask one of the ladies. "Something to cool your throat, sir?" he would ask a dancing gentleman. The Prince was everywhere. The masked ball was, without a doubt, the most elegant social event of any year.

Time will fly when one is enjoying oneself. So it came as a shock when the strange clock began to strike the hour of midnight. The chimes seemed louder than before. By the fourth chime, the musicians had stopped playing altogether. The dancers turned in surprise and then in uneasiness. The sound of the chimes, pouring from the seventh room at the end, echoed along the walls of the other rooms.

Perhaps it was just that everyone was standing so still. Or perhaps it was that everything was so quiet when the last chime had sounded. But suddenly there was a low murmur of surprise and talk throughout the first room. For there, standing in the middle of the floor was a masked figure no one had seen before. As more and more of the guests looked, more and more gasps of horror were heard.

It was true that the Prince had instructed his guests to dress in all manner of bizarre costumes—from the beautiful to the strange to the ridiculous. But this—this was not to be believed!

The tall, masked figure stood alone in the middle of the room, dressed in a flowing cloak of darkest gray. The mask he wore to cover his face looked like that of a skeleton or a corpse, as though this strange figure had just risen from the grave. Now such a costume might have been tolerated, except for one thing. Covering the skeleton's mask were bright red marks—the marks of blood, the scarlet marks of the Red Death!

Suddenly, Prince Prospero, who had been in another room, came in to see what had caused the silence. When he looked at the masked figure, his face twisted in rage. "Who dares to in-

sult me and my guests in this manner?" he cried. "Who dares to bring even the thought of this horror into my castle?"

Then the Prince looked around. "Seize him!" he shouted to some of the guests. "We will unmask him, and he will be hanged at sunrise for this outrage!"

A few of the guests moved forward as the deathly figure slowly approached the Prince. But then they shrank back against the wall, frozen with a strange fear. Then, untouched, the masked figure walked slowly down the line of ballrooms, until he stood at the entrance of the seventh room.

By this time, Prince Prospero had recovered from his shock. He hurried through the rooms, drawing out his dagger as he went.

The masked figure turned as the Prince approached him. Suddenly, the guests heard a sharp cry. The dagger fell from the Prince's hand. And, the life already gone from his body, Prince Prospero fell to the floor.

For a few moments, everyone stood shocked and unmoving. Then a few of the guests came to their senses and ran into the black ballroom. The strange guest stood before the huge ebony clock. The guests rushed at him, their hands clutching

at the gray cloak and the deathlike mask, pulling them away.

No one spoke a word. No one uttered a sound. For beneath the cloak and the mask was nothing. Nothing at all. *No one.* The cloak and the mask fell silently to the floor.

One by one, in unspeakable horror, the guests came to realize what was in the room. The servants and musicians realized it as well. Like a thief in the night, the Red Death had come. The castle walls had not been able to keep it out.

Here and there, people began to cry out in pain, and fall to the floor in dizziness. Within half an hour, the floors of the great ballrooms were covered with blood and littered with bodies.

When the last person had died in agony, the great ebony clock stood lifeless and still. The flames from the huge torches on the walls flickered and died.

Now, darkness and decay and the Red Death ruled everywhere.

Bluebeard

In a time long ago, there lived a very rich man. He lived in a great gray castle high on a hill. The castle was filled with objects of silver and gold. The furniture was made of rare wood from faraway lands. And the rich man rode in a coach that sparkled with rubies.

But rich as he was, the man had no friends and no wife. For he was hideously ugly, and most disagreeable. His ugliness was made worse by an enormous blue beard that framed his face. And so he was known as Bluebeard.

There was nothing Bluebeard wanted more than a wife. But all the girls and women ran away if he so much as looked toward them.

One of Bluebeard's neighbors was a fine woman who had two beautiful daughters and two sons.

"I ask for the hand of one of your daughters in marriage," Bluebeard told the woman one day. "I will leave it up to you to choose which one."

Now in spite of Bluebeard's frightful looks, the fine woman was flattered by his proposal, because he was so rich. But in truth, neither of the daughters wanted to marry him. They didn't like him, and thought him dreadfully ugly. They liked him even less because of a rumor that Bluebeard had already had several wives. And no one seemed to know what had become of them.

Bluebeard thought that perhaps one of the daughters would change her mind if they became better acquainted. So he invited the woman and her daughters and some of their friends to his castle for a week. Never had the daughters and their friends seen such parties and such wealth. They hunted and fished and walked during the day. They feasted and danced and laughed through the night.

All during the week, Bluebeard was most charming and polite. He joked with the daughters and impressed them with his fine manners.

In fact, he impressed the youngest daughter so much that she began to think he was not quite so ugly. Was it possible his beard was not quite as blue as she thought? He really wasn't such a bad fellow after all, she decided. And, of course, he *was* very rich.

By the end of the week, the youngest daughter said that she would become Bluebeard's wife. And before long they were married. The wedding was grand, and people were invited from far and wide. Bluebeard was pleasant and courteous. And the youngest daughter began to think that, indeed, his beard was not blue at all.

About a month after the wedding, Bluebeard told his young wife, "I must leave for six weeks on important business. Invite your friends to the castle while I am gone. And enjoy yourself."

Then he gave her the keys to the castle, saying, "This is the key to the storeroom where I keep my treasure. Here is the key to my strongbox, which holds my gold and silver. Here is the key to my jewel box. Open what you will. But this I warn you. *Do not use this little key.* It opens the small room at the end of the passageway on the ground floor. I forbid you to open this door. If you do, your punishment will be more terrible than you can imagine."

The young wife promised to obey Bluebeard's instructions. Then he set out on his journey.

No sooner had Bluebeard's coach disappeared into the forest than the guests began to arrive. None of them had visited the castle since the wedding. In truth, they were afraid of the young girl's husband.

Soon the guests were wandering about the castle. They poked into the great storerooms and admired the gold and silver. They stared with

wide eyes at the precious jewels, and they tried on diamond necklaces and earrings. And even though they thought Bluebeard was very ugly, they decided that the young wife was lucky to live amid all this splendor and wealth.

But the wife could hardly wait for her guests to leave. She was longing to examine the small room at the end of the passageway on the ground floor. She could think of nothing else—even though Bluebeard had forbidden her to open the door.

As soon as the castle was quiet, she ran down the back stairway, nearly breaking her neck in her haste. Breathless, she reached the small door. A sudden chill came over her as she held the key to the lock. Should she open it? She remembered Bluebeard's words.

But her curiosity could not be ignored. With a trembling hand, she thrust the key into the lock and opened the little door.

At first she could see nothing, for the room was dark. She opened the shutters so she could look about. Then she gasped. So frightful was the sight before her that her heart seemed to stop! Blood was everywhere. And against one wall there were several ebony coffins covered with dust and cobwebs.

She knew at once what was in the coffins, and

she was filled with horror. "The other wives of Bluebeard!" she gasped. "He has murdered them all!"

She fled from the room in terror, and tried to lock the door. But her hand was shaking so much that the key fell to the floor. She picked it up, locked the door, and fled upstairs. Her shock was so great that she did not look at the little key for a long time. When she did, her horror grew twice as great as before. The little key was stained with blood!

She tried to wash the key with soap. But the blood was still there. Then she scoured it with sand and stone. The blood was still there. She did not know that the key was magical. If the blood was washed from one side, it appeared on the other. It would never come clean again.

The poor girl was too frightened to think. And in the next second she nearly fainted again. For she heard her husband's coach pulling up to the castle.

In a few minutes Bluebeard called out, "Where is my lovely wife?"

She hid her trembling hands, and went to greet him. "Are you back so soon?" she asked.

Bluebeard told her that he had received a let-ter along the road telling him to return home for a

more important business matter. The young wife tried to act as though she were glad to see him. But she only grew more nervous, and the evening seemed to last forever.

The next morning, at breakfast, Bluebeard asked his wife for the castle keys. As she handed them to him, she could not hide her nervousness. Her hands trembled so much that Bluebeard immediately guessed what had happened.

"Where is the key to the little room, my dear?" he asked. "Why is it not among the rest?"

"Oh, isn't it there?" asked his wife, in a soft voice. "I must have left it upstairs on my table."

And Bluebeard responded, "Be so kind as to fetch it for me."

The young girl tried to delay as much as possible. But after many excuses, she was forced to bring the key to her husband. Bluebeard looked at it, and asked, "How is it, my good wife, that there is blood upon this key?"

"I do not know," she replied. Her face was as pale as death.

"You do not know!" roared Bluebeard. "But I *do* know. You disobeyed me. You entered the forbidden room. Very well, madam, you shall visit it once more. And this time, you shall take your place among the others who are there."

26

At that, the terrified wife threw herself at her husband's feet and begged his forgiveness. But it was all in vain.

"You have disobeyed me, and you must die!" Bluebeard said.

The young wife's eyes filled with tears. Then she begged, "If I must die, at least give me time for my prayers." She looked so beautiful and sorrowful that the very sight of her would have melted a heart of stone.

But Bluebeard's heart was far harder than stone.

"I will give you one quarter of an hour," he said, "and not a moment more." Then he left her.

As soon as she was alone, the young wife called to a servant. "Go quickly to the top of the tower," she said. "My brothers are to pay a visit to the castle today. See if they are coming. If you see them, give a signal to hasten."

The servant ran to the tower. In a few minutes, the wife called, "Do you see anyone coming?"

And the servant replied, "I see nothing but the sun that burns, and the grass that waves."

Then Bluebeard, who was waiting downstairs with a great sword in his hand, called in a loud voice, "Your time is through. Come down at once!"

"Just one moment more," called his wife. Then she called, "My servant, do you see anyone coming?"

And the servant answered, "I see nothing but the sun that burns, and the grass that waves."

Bluebeard called again, "Come down this instant!"

"But a moment more," cried his wife. Then once more she asked the servant, "Do you see anyone coming?"

This time the servant replied, "I see a great cloud of dust moving this way."

"Is it my brothers?"

"Alas, dear mistress, it is but a flock of sheep."

Now Bluebeard screamed in a terrible voice, "Come down this instant, or I will come up for you!"

"I am coming," his wife called. Then she cried to her servant, "Do you see anyone coming?"

"I see two horsemen," the servant replied, "but they are yet a great way off."

"They are my brothers!" the young wife cried. "Make the signal for them to hasten!"

This time Bluebeard screamed so loudly that the castle walls shook. The terrified girl ran down the stairs to him. She threw herself at his feet, weeping.

"You must die," said Bluebeard. And then, with one hand, he lifted her long, flowing hair. With the other he raised his heavy sword.

"Give me just one moment before I die," his wife begged.

"Not a moment more," said Bluebeard, and he raised his sword higher.

At that very instant, the castle gates were thrown open, and in rushed the two brothers. They flew at Bluebeard, waving their swords. Bluebeard quickly tried to make his escape. But the brothers caught him and killed him with their swords. Bluebeard was dead.

Bluebeard had no heirs, so his wife inherited all his riches. She gave some of the money to her sister, who soon married a gentleman who loved her. She used some of it to buy captains' commissions for her brothers. Not long afterwards, she herself married a very handsome and kind gentleman. And in time she forgot about the terrible days she had passed with Bluebeard.

The Thief on Tower Bridge

In a faraway land lived a widow and her son. He was a clever lad, and she loved him dearly. The widow saved all her money so that her son might learn a good trade when he was grown. But when he became a young man, he told his mother that he had only one desire. He wanted to become a thief.

His mother was horrified. "How can you wish for such an evil thing?" she cried. "Don't you know that all the thieves of this land end their lives by hanging from the Tower Bridge?" Then she began to weep.

The son did not want to listen to his mother cry. So he said, "I will make this promise to you. The trade that I will follow shall be the first trade you hear named when you leave the market tomorrow."

The widow felt better after that. The next day after leaving the market, she began to walk home through the village. But her son had hidden himself in the bushes. As she passed by, he whispered, "Thief! Thief!"

The widow did not recognize her son's voice.

She became very frightened and sad. Now she knew that her son would truly become a thief.

A few days later, the widow said to her son, "I have been thinking about what you have told me. It grieves me that you wish to follow such an evil trade. But I do not want you to end your life hanging from the Tower Bridge. So if you must become a thief, you must learn from a good one. There is no better thief than the Purple Rogue. He has been stealing for years, and no one has been able to catch him."

"I will become *better* than he is," said the son. "I will become the best thief in the land. And since the Purple Rogue has a color in his name, I shall have one too. From now on, I shall call myself the Gray Thief."

And so, for many weeks after that, the Gray Thief met with the Purple Rogue every evening to learn the dark secrets of his chosen trade. The young man was very clever, and he learned quickly and well.

One evening, the Purple Rogue said, "So you think you are ready to take part in a real robbery. This will be a test of how well you have learned. And, in the bargain, I will bet you one-hundred silver pieces that you will fail."

"I will take that bet," said the Gray Thief.

"Listen carefully," said the Purple Rogue. "Next week there is to be a grand wedding. The bridegroom's uncle is a rich farmer. He has decided to send a fat sheep to the young couple as a wedding present. You must steal the sheep from the shepherd who brings it to town."

"It is done," said the Gray Thief.

The next week, the Gray Thief ran to the wood where the shepherd would pass. He took off one of his shoes and covered it with mud. Then he dropped it on the path and hid behind a rock.

When the shepherd came by with the sheep, he saw the shoe. "It is dirty," he said. "If only I had the other shoe, it would be worth cleaning this one." At that, he left the shoe, and went on.

The Gray Thief picked up the shoe and took a short cut through the woods. He dropped his other shoe in the shepherd's path. Soon the shepherd came by.

"This must be the mate to the first shoe," said the shepherd. "I must go back and get it." So the shepherd tied the sheep to a tree and ran back for the first shoe.

Quickly, the Gray Thief put on both his shoes, untied the sheep and took it to the home of the Purple Rogue. And since he had won the bet, he collected one-hundred silver pieces.

When the farmer heard that the sheep had been lost, he was very annoyed. But he sent the shepherd to town with a goat. As the shepherd was leading the goat through the wood, the Gray Thief began to baa like a sheep.

"That sounds like the sheep I lost," said the shepherd. "The farmer will be very glad that I found it again." So the shepherd tied the goat to a tree and went off looking for the sheep.

The Gray Thief hopped out from his hiding place, untied the goat, and took it to the home of the Purple Rogue.

The farmer was really angry when he heard that both his sheep and his goat were now lost. But he still had to send his nephew a wedding present. So this time he sent the shepherd to town with a cow, telling him to be extra careful.

"We will get the cow, too," said the Gray Thief.

"Just how do you plan to do that?" asked the Purple Rogue.

"Come with me to the wood. When the shepherd passes, you baa like a sheep. I will go in the other direction and bleat like a goat."

As the shepherd led the cow through the wood, he heard a loud baa from one direction and a loud bleat from the other.

"That must be the lost sheep and goat," said the shepherd. "The farmer will be very happy if I find them."

The shepherd tied up the cow and went off to look for the sheep and the goat. When he was gone, the Gray Thief and the Purple Rogue stole the cow. The poor shepherd was beaten severely when he returned to the farmer.

After that, the Gray Thief became bolder and bolder. He stole almost anything, and he was very good at it.

"I am a better thief than you are," he said to the Purple Rogue.

"You are good, I will say that—but you will never be better than I am," said the Purple Rogue.

This angered the Gray Thief, but he did not say anything more.

One night, the Gray Thief and the Purple Rogue were returning from a robbery. They passed a gallows that had been built in the town square. No one was in sight.

"It looks like someone is going to be hanged," said the Gray Thief. "Let's take a closer look. I've never seen a gallows before."

The Gray Thief put the rope around his neck and told the Purple Rogue to pull on the other

end. "I want to see how it feels," he said. The Purple Rogue pulled the rope a little, and then let the Gray Thief down.

"Actually, you wouldn't believe it, but it's rather pleasant to be swinging in the air," said the Gray Thief.

"Well, let me try, if it's so nice," said the Purple Rogue. He put the rope around his neck, and the Gray Thief pulled on the other end. He pulled and pulled until the Purple Rogue was swinging high in the air.

"Didn't I tell you it was pleasant?" laughed the Gray Thief. And he watched until the Purple Rogue was dead.

Then the young man went to the wife of the Purple Rogue, and said, "Your husband is dead, but I am a better thief than he was, so why don't you marry me?"

But the woman was horrified. She would not marry him and threatened to call the sheriff.

After that, the Gray Thief roamed the countryside, and stole from everybody. He grew more bold and more wicked. Finally, the King sent out a band of soldiers to catch him. But the Gray Thief crept up on the soldiers when they were sleeping, and killed them all.

Now the King asked the advice of his wise

council. They told him to hold a large ball and invite all the people of the countryside. The Gray Thief was so bold that surely he would come and ask the Princess to dance.

So the King held a huge ball, and everyone was invited. Sure enough, the Gray Thief did come, and he asked the Princess to dance. Then one of the members of the council managed to place a small black dot beneath his ear. But, the Gray Thief realized what had happened. So after dancing with the Princess, he stole a bottle of black ink from the council and put small black dots on the faces of twenty other young men at the ball.

When the ball was over, the King ordered all the doors to be locked. Then his soldiers searched for the young man with the black dot on his face. What they found were twenty-one young men with black dots on their faces.

"This thief is very clever," said the King. "He is more clever than my wise council. If he will show himself to me, I will grant whatever he wishes."

The Gray Thief stepped forward. "I am the clever thief," he said boldly. "And what I wish is to marry your lovely daughter."

The Princess was quite taken with the clever young man, and so she agreed to the marriage.

The very next day the Princess and the Gray Thief were married. "I wish that my mother could see me at this moment," said the Gray Thief with a smile.

A few days after the wedding, the Gray Thief and the Princess were out walking. They came to a shallow river, and over the river was a small bridge.

"What bridge is this?" asked the Gray Thief.

"It is called Tower Bridge," said the young bride.

"I have heard of it," the Gray Thief said. "In fact, my mother often told me that I would hang from it."

"If you wish," said the Princess with a laugh, "we can make her words come true! Let us tie my handkerchief around your ankle. You hang down from the bridge, and I will hold on. Then, when you see your mother, you can tell her that she was right after all! That will be a good laugh on her!"

"A splendid idea!" said the Gray Thief. "But you are not strong enough to hold me up."

"Oh yes I am," said the Princess. "Come, I'll show you."

The Gray Thief was always ready to accept a dare, so he agreed. He tied the handkerchief

around his ankle and lowered himself over the bridge. The Princess held on to the other end of the handkerchief.

"You see, I am strong enough to hold you," cried the Princess.

"Yes, I have to agree that you are," called the Gray Thief, who was hanging upside-down. "Now, pull me up."

At that moment, a great cry came from the castle, and a servant ran down the path. "The castle is on fire! The castle is on fire!" the servant called.

In her panic, the Princess let go of the handkerchief. Her husband fell into the river below, striking his head on a huge rock. He died in an instant.

And the widow's words to her son had come true after all.